DIRECT MAIL
IN A DIGITAL WORLD

PAT PENDERGAST

FOREWARD

The "Digital Revolution" has sucked the life out of the free market system. Today, a vast number of consumers have "Attention Deficit Disorder." It is getting more difficult everyday to get the attention of anyone to effectively present and sell a product or service.

As business professionals we are being told to focus our efforts towards online marketing. We are getting pressured to have "state of the art" websites. We are being told, "Email Marketing is King!" We are the opposite of "cool" if we aren't connected with an umbilical chord to all the major social media sites. Some, so-called, "experts" have the nerve to say without a social media presence a business will not survive. To all this I say, "Take a seat!"

I have made a very successful and comfortable living by adopting the opposing strategies that are "hip, cool and trendy." I teach entrepreneurs all over America to do the opposite of what everyone else is doing to stand out and get noticed. I am, and always will be, an advocate of "Old School" marketing strategies and techniques. They have worked in the past. They are working today. They will work until the end of days.

I'm talking about the "Old School" marketing methods of *direct mail*. Postcards, newsletters, sales letters, notes of appreciation and anything else you put a stamp on to have arrive at a customer's doorstep.

Direct mail is a critical component to a successful and sustainable business plan. Consumers are craving to be entertained and surprised. Consumers want to sit down with a cup of coffee and read all the details about the offer you have. Consumers want to be shown some respect by showing up with printed materials they can read without having the glow of the computer screen leading them to today's headache.

The brilliance of *direct mail* is it can bring you new customers, keep current customers informed, entertained and happy, and help solidify any efforts, online or offline, by furthering the sales process. Consumers want to know you care enough to spend a few extra dollars to show up in their mailbox and not take the cheap way out by sending an email.

Navigating today's world of *direct mail* can be daunting. That is why you should be congratulated for taking the time to read this well thought out publication by one of the foremost experts of *direct mail*, Pat Pendergast.

I had the pleasure of being introduced to Pat back in 2006. Pat has not only showed me time after time why he is a true expert and strategist when it comes to *direct mail*, but he does it with a straightforward, uncomplicated and careful thought-out process.

Every business professional serious about creating a profitable and sustainable business needs to incorporate *direct mail* into his/her marketing plan. There is no one better to advise you and guide you through the process than Pat.

By the time you finish reading this carefully thought-out book, you will know why Pat is my #1, go-to expert whenever I want to develop a *direct mail* campaign that will create a profitable, winning campaign. I am proud to have Pat on my team, not only because he is a consummate professional, but because I have the privilege to call him my friend.

Pat, thank you for taking all the time and effort to put together this comprehensive, step-by-step guide to help business professionals understand the complicated world of *direct mail*. You are a gift to the business world.

Today, choose to be extraordinary!

Kevin Kowalke

Founder - **Thursday Morning Thing** (Milwaukee, WI)

"The Place Where World Class Entrepreneurs Train"

Table of Contents

INTRODUCTION

When initially writing this book, I thought it would be about the life and times of Pat Pendergast. Then, I realized that would not be helpful to anyone. So, I decided I would share my secrets about *direct mail* and *direct mail marketing*, which have been my success strategy for business growth and profitability ("Snail mail" for you technology types out there) Don't let it fool you; used correctly, *direct mail* will continue to make you money time and time again.

In these days of internet marketing, *direct mail* has been given a bad rap. Everyone is caught up in the hype of Twitter, Facebook, Pinterest, and all the other electronic noise coming day after day. Consumers are bombarded with over 5,000 electronic advertising messages over the course of a day. How can one business stand out in the midst of all this noise? Unless you have a million dollar pay-per-click budget you are bound to get lost and never found.

One of the fundamental flaws of a *direct mail* campaign is the enduring ability of the sender. This is called "market stamina" by a good friend of mine, Tim Schmidt, a marketing success story himself. Most *direct mail* failures are attributed to being one and done. A small business owner is experiencing a slow-down in business and wants to send out a quick mailer to get the phone ringing. Wrong approach! They should have been sending *direct mail* to their clients and prospects a long time ago. A one-time shotgun method just does not work. You need to be consistent and test it over and over again. You need to get in front of your customers and prospects at least once a month. Inside, I will talk about a retail client of mine that uses only *direct mail* to get their customers in the door numerous times over the year.

I will share with you my successes and failures with *direct mail*. Let's not re-invent the wheel. Use the methods and tactics that will get your clients to buy from you and keep buying from you. I promise you that I will not hold back on anything. Inside is the good, the bad, and the ugly.

I encourage you to read this book from start to finish. Then, keep it in your office as a reference that you can go back to when you are putting together your *direct mail marketing* campaign. I assure you; it will save you money and time.

I wish you continued success in your business, career, and life.

"If a man writes a book, let him set down only what he knows. I have guesses enough of my own..." -Johan Wolfgang Von Goethe

Let's get started...

Chapter 1
HOW TO GET STARTED WITH DIRECT MAIL

My printing career began over 30 years ago as a printing press operator fresh out of technical school. Over the years I have managed a print shop, purchased a printing franchise, and have become a *direct mail* marketing entrepreneur. Currently, I help clients make money in their businesses using *direct mail*. I have been actively marketing my printing and mailing business for over 25 years using *direct mail*. Needing to separate myself from the burden of a franchise owner, I started marketing myself as a *direct mail* expert. My *direct mail* marketing material helps spread the word that I can help my clients and prospects increase their marketing dollar return on investment. In showing my clients and prospects that I use *direct mail*, I have gained credibility in the industry.

I wrote this book as a roadmap for businesses to get through the methods of *direct mail* and marketing. I will share what I currently use, and also tell you what hasn't worked for me. Everything I talk about in this book is something I have tried or have had a client test. You can learn from my testing to help shorten your learning curve and be successful faster. Some of my methods will work and give you the results you want. Some may not fit as well for your type of business. Either way, I want to give you everything I have tried so you have all the options available to you. I have successfully used postcards, newsletters, email, blogs, websites, salespeople and a book. Currently, I am using all of these methods except a salesperson, which may come later. I have written this book for you, my clients, and prospects. This book is my business card.

Why would I want to give away my "secrets" of marketing success? Two reasons… I want you to succeed in business and in life. We are not in competition with each other and the universe is large enough for all of us. 99% of the people reading this will not do anything shown in this book. Some may try a few things and have wonderful success. Great, that is what I want to see! Some may try and abandon it with a "he didn't know what he was talking about." I say keep looking and testing an idea to find out what does work. Searching for a working method may include ideas from other people or industries. You have to completely embrace testing an idea to find the method to work for you. A friend of mine, Tim Schmidt, owner of a very successful online business (uscca.com) recently gave me some valuable advice. He said I need to have marketing stamina. I need to have the guts to test and test again. I've perfected the product; I just need to continually test ideas and measure the results. This is the secret sauce.

I have been to several seminars in recent years costing thousands of dollars to attend. Hundreds of people attend these seminars, and I can count on one hand how many people actually implemented the ideas and directions given. I think it is human nature to look for an "easy money" idea or method. In each of these seminars, the methods given would take a lot of hard work to get proven results. Once people realized the amount of work involved, they either abandoned the idea shortly after starting or never started at all. I was in a very expensive seminar in 2005 with over 150 people in attendance. The moderator gave us line by line instructions and directions on implementing a *direct mail* campaign. After 3 years, only 3 people continued using the program. Of the 3, two had success, me being one of them. No one else tried it or worked it. This just shows you the majority of people are looking for a "get rich quick scheme".

I'm all about the 20 year overnight success of someone. I'm not worried about giving away my "secrets" because the size of the market is so vast you won't directly compete with one another. I have been in business for quite a long time and I find very few people that are consistently testing and marketing their company with proven results.

The truth is regular mail, although simple, is a time-honored tradition respected by business leaders and the general consumer alike. Both at the office and at home, when the mail arrives, it is one of the most important times of the day. It is safe to say most individuals would be much more pleased with receiving a paper greeting card than an electronic greeting card (e-card). With this book I'm here to help you leverage your business with *direct mail*.

SUMMARY

- *Consistent direct mail works!*

- *The Universe is large enough for all of us.*

- *Don't re-invent the wheel. Use my experience to ramp up your campaign quickly.*

- *Test, test, test, find what works for you!*

- *Marketing Stamina……. you need it!*

- *Trust the Secret Sauce.*

- *Send a card, not an email!*

Chapter 2
TOP OF MIND AWARENESS
& CREATING YOUR OWN LUCK

If you are selling a non-impulse product or service, such as a car, house painting, or kitchen remodeling, you want to be "top of mind" when a customer decides to buy. Consider the car market for a moment. Consumers are bombarded by so many car commercials, it is hard to separate them all. The advertisers push quality, loyalty, and gadgets. They try to connect a car brand with a successful program or famous person. As an example, Ford caught my eye recently with Mike Rowe from the Discovery Channel's "Dirty Jobs." One company doing a great job of "top of mind" advertising is "College Pro Painters." They market in newspapers, flyers, inserts and go door to door. Their timing is spot on as well. They hit it hard in early spring; thus, coming to mind when I need my house painted. Another example is remodeling services. I'm sure you can think of a local company selling remodeling services. You may have heard them on the radio, seen them in the newspaper, or on television. They are getting their name out there for when you are in the market for their product. However, "top of mind" awareness can be an expensive method of marketing. Trying to get your name out to the masses with a shotgun approach is not the most cost effective for most businesses. Targeted *direct mail* is your solution.

Here are some research numbers from Chilton about how long it takes consumers to make a large purchase decision:

15% - Bought within the first three months

24% - Bought within four to six months

34% - Bought within seven to twelve months

27%- Bought more than twelve months later

These are amazing numbers for consideration. This is why so many small businesses give up on marketing so quickly. They don't realize the time it takes for a consumer to make a decision. Unless you have a steep discount with a short purchase period (low profit), you may not see results for months. "Top of mind" awareness allows you to own the space your product or service occupies in your prospect's mind. Be "top of mind", and when they're ready to buy, they'll come to you first.

Today's buyer uses an information-oriented decision process involving the following:

Gathering of information

Reviewing alternatives (great time to show testimonials)

Choosing one alternative

Evaluating the decision after the fact

Your service or product needs to get in at the beginning of the process, when the consumer is gathering facts relating to her/his problem or need… AND STAY THERE! Once you have identified your best prospects, stay in touch through mail, email, phone, etc.

Hang in there. The decision processes takes longer than you think. Most small business owners are very impatient and move on too quickly before giving a method a chance.

⚙️ TOOLBOX TIP

Want to see a sample of a 175-Day Campaign?

Go to www.patpendergast.com, register if you are a first time customer, and enter the number "175" in Pendy's Toolbox.

Ideas

Ideas are great. We can't live without them, but you need to take an idea and implement it. Work it, and run it through the time it deserves. I have heard many ideas and have come up with a few of my own, but without action an idea is worthless. You need to put an idea into action and give it the time needed to succeed or fail. I have read many websites extolling how to come up with ideas, but never sharing how to put the idea into the universe as something measurable. Many people never get past the idea stage. True success comes when the idea is implemented and it works. Too many ideas can cause paralysis. I have seen this over and over again in my business owner's mastermind group. Many great ideas are shared, but few implemented; thus, little to no success is achieved. You have to try it to see if it works!

Here are three ideas (considered bad at one time) from one person, Wayne Huizenga, that turned into success stories:

Waste Management

When he was a garbage collection manager, he decided to build his own trash collecting business.

Blockbuster

The next big idea was to rent movie videos in malls and free-standing building. Wayne sold it at it's peak. As we all know, Blockbuster did not adjust to the market fast enough.

AutoNation

His last "bad idea" was a national chain of used car outlets.

Here is one of my ideas that I use to this day: Every box that I deliver finished printing to my customers has the name of my company, phone number, email, and website address on it. The reason for this is the person that placed the original order may no longer be with the company when it is time to re-order. No need to look up where you bought your printing, it's right on the box. Next time you get a box from Amazon, look on the outside of the box. Amazon is all over it. What is a simple idea, just needs to be implemented.

HOT TIP

Add your picture in your email signature!

Email me at Pat@MillPM.com with the name "Wise Stamp" in the subject line and I will reply back with my email signature and instructions.

Luck

Luck is what happens when preparation meets opportunity.

Let me give you an example: You have been mailing your newsletter to prospects for over a year. One day you get a call from someone on your newsletter list to come in to discuss a project they have. Would you call this luck? I would, but with one caveat. The "luck" was created by making contact with this person for over a year. You were in the right place at the right time by being visual every month. When they were ready, on their time, they remembered you and reached out to make the purchase.

Now if you hadn't been sending your newsletter on a regular basis and only sent it once or twice in a year, you may not have gotten the phone call. Random mailings are not effective. Consistently staying in front of a prospect will give you better results. You will be the lucky one!

Here is another story illustrating timing (luck). Years ago my print shop was in a strip mall on a busy street. I had a rather large sign on the outside of the building, not much different than the other signs on the building. One day a person walks in the door and says "I didn't even know a print shop was in this mall". This particular day he had a need for printing and saw the sign above our shop. He had been driving by my shop for months, if not years. The day came when he had a need and he noticed my sign. He subconsciously saw my sign, but because he didn't need printing at the time, he never really noticed it. The moral is, you create your luck by preparing the client to think of you when they are ready to buy. You can send mailings and offers until the cows come home, but you won't hear from a consumer until they are ready to buy!

As an entrepreneur, I have found myself envious of a successful person's "luck." In my heart though, I know the odds are this successful person worked very hard to get where they are. In fact

I use it as an opportunity to learn more about them and see how and why they became successful. I learn more from this exercise than just wishing I had their luck. I can guarantee you their success didn't fall from the sky.

As I write this the Olympics are going on. My family is glued to the television every night watching these amazing athletes. What we don't see are the hours and hours of hard work these athletes put in to get to this elite level. Each of them has created their own luck. Hard work, perseverance, and discipline in the face of impossible odds have brought these athletes from all over the world to compete at the highest levels.

Another example of how preparation meets luck comes from my business owner's mastermind group. The group meets monthly and is composed of 8 business owners getting together to brainstorm business success strategies. The group fee is priced high enough to make sure members are serious about contributing. Three members have come out of these mastermind groups I participate in and are having million dollar months. A newer member of this mastermind group is Sonny Ahuja. He is an Internet guru selling perfume online and also specializing in website development, SEO, and social media.

Sonny has been in the mastermind group for about a year now and has been working really hard on finding ways to sell websites to certain niches. One of his niches is home remodelers. He began sending the remodelers mailings and offering them a seminar. He didn't do any phone follow-up, thus; was not very successful. Sonny is from India and has an accent making him hard to understand sometimes, making cold calls unsuccessful. Sonny brought his frustrations to the mastermind group and everyone gave him ideas and honest feedback. Sonny soon realized his expertise and the leverage with the outsourced India market gave him an advantage. He simply needed to share this with the potential client. Sonny's "luck" has turned around and he is now knocking it out of the park.

One great thing about a mastermind group is you get tons of ideas and feedback. The key is being part of the correct group for your business and level of success. Over the years people have come and gone from my own group. There are two individuals who leveraged their membership to become very successful; Tim Schmidt (usconcealedcarry.com) and Dr. Rick Schaefer (kneespecialistsofwisconsin.com). Both spent 1-2 years in the group before moving on. While in the group, each implemented the ideas created; thus, gaining traction with their success. Tim now belongs to a mastermind group with a yearly membership fee of $25,000. These owners look for ideas and business companions mirroring the level of success they wish to achieve. Consider where you are getting your ideas from before expending lots of energy. Surrounding yourself with people above your level of success will help you stretch and grow.

Belonging to a mastermind group can also help you find resources for your own business. For Example, I hired Sonny to do some work on my Welcome Card USA website. He was a great asset. I also became a perfect testimonial for Sonny's website business. Then one day my washing machine broke. I was feverishly looking for the phone number of an appliance repairman friend of mine. I went online, and after some extended struggles, I finally found it. Through this process, I recognized his online business page had a very poor page ranking. Heck, they didn't even show up on a Google search. I asked Sonny if he would be interested in working with me to help my friend out. I brought him to the presentation and closed the deal. His expertise and credibility tipped the scales in our favor. My friend launched a newly optimized website recently and can now be found in the first several pages of Google. Now, in addition to offering *direct mail* services, I also offer website SEO in conjunction with Sonny. It has expanded my customer base and increased my "luck." The same luck can come to you! Time + Effort = Luck!

Direct Mail Still Works

Yes, overall mail volume is down. Yes, there's flight by consumers and foolish marketers away from "snail-mail." This may be true so determine your course of action with *direct mail* marketing.

DIRECT MAIL'S DEATH CONTINUES TO BE EXAGGERATED.

Here are the top 50 users of *direct mail* in 2011:

Citigroup	*Consumers Union*
DirecTV	*NRA*
GEICO	*Suarez Corp.*
Mutual of Omaha	*March of Dimes*
Time Inc.	*Omaha Steaks*
American Red Cross	*Disabled American Veterans*
Salvation Army	*World Wildlife Fund*
New York Times	*Paralyzed Veterans of America*
Hearst Magazines	*Rodale*

Reader's Digest Assoc.	United Service Organization
AARP	Sierra Club
Bose	Smile Train
Dow Jones	Highlights for Children
American Heart Assoc.	Arbor Day Foundation
St. Jude Hospital	Nat'l Breast Cancer Coalition
The Economist Group	Int'l Master Publishers
PBS	Connect America
Publishers Clearinghouse	The Bradford Group
Hachette Filipacchi Media	Boardroom
Nat'l Geographic Society	Cone Nast
Habitat for Humanity	Littleton Rare Coins
Leukemia Society	Luscxiana Health
N. Amer. Mbshp. Group	Premier Bathrooms
Sloan-Kettering Cancer Soc.	AAA
NRDC	Meredith Corp. Humane Soc.

46% of this top-50 list is made up of non-profits, who cannot live without *direct mail*. Media/publishing companies (including info-marketers) held steady at 30%. Merchandisers surged from 2% to 10% - higher if you include Omaha Steaks. New to the top 50 in 2012: DirecTV, GEICO, Bose, NRA, Premier Bathrooms. This list excludes catalogs.

Let's discuss some of the members of this list. GEICO is a company you see advertising on TV incessantly. They advertise on radio too, yet they are one of the largest *direct mail* users. Notice how many non-profits there are, including two of the largest charities: SALVATION ARMY and AMERICAN RED CROSS. BOSE and OHAHA STEAKS have retail distribution and robust online marketing, yet both rank in the top 50 users of *direct mail*. RODALE and BOARDROOM are two of the largest info-marketers in the industry. Brian Kurtz from Boardroom is a list wizard. Ask him how quickly Boardroom would shrink if it abandoned *direct mail* for online. PREMIER BATHROOMS is in print, TV, and online, but also on top 50 *direct mailer* list. *Direct mail* generates leads across all age demographics. Direct marketing champion Ben Suarez, best known for Amish heaters, uses print ads everywhere. You see them in USA TODAY, while some you may see in Farm Bureau journals. Suarez also sells health books and water purifiers with this combined marketing approach. His companies generate billions of dollars in revenue yearly. *Direct mail* is a key component to his success.

🔥 HOT TIP

Go to Geico.com and get an auto quote from them.

Be sure to include your mailing address. Geico will send you a series of *direct mail* pieces if you don't purchase online. Even the online guys use *direct mail*.

IMPORTANT FACT: the median revenue for these top 50 mailers INCREASED by $50-million this year vs. same months of 2010. Can it be coincidence the top 50 mailers are creating sales increases despite an economic recession?

1. If you are going to use *direct mail*, at minimum you want to be on the mailing lists of the companies on this top-50 list. Learn from them, especially from the companies selling comparable products or services to your customers. If running a non-profit, you have to give to every charity listed here to be sure you get all their mail to study. If you're an info-marketer, you have to buy from Boardroom and Rodale to get their mail. These are the 50 companies able to use more *direct mail* than all others, so their output must be collected, analyzed and emulated in your own tests. If there is a company on this list with significant commonality to what you sell or whom you sell to, you must become an expert on this company.

2. If you are not going to use *direct mail*, know you are ignoring the media these companies rely upon. These 50 companies have increased their sales significantly year after year. Are you sure you don't want to reconsider your decision?

3. Beware of popular talk amongst your peers about media; consider facts, reality, and real leaders' behaviors.

4. Test, test, test. This the only way you are going to get the cold hard facts. Successful marketers are always testing to maximize results.

All of the top 50 companies I listed have shown that *direct mail* has worked for them for years and years. They have tested and refined their methods to get better results, even during an economic slowdown. You may not be as large as these companies are, but you can use their methods to produce the results you need.

SUMMARY

- *Top of Mind Awareness, timing is everything.*

- *Create your "Luck".*

- *Percentages don't lie, people take time to buy.*

- *Understand the buyer's decision process.*

- *Implement your ideas.*

- *Put your name and picture on everything.*

- *Luck meets opportunity with long hours and hard work.*

- *Find a Mastermind group to join.*

- *Large companies are using direct mail.*

- *Get on the mailing list of direct mail marketers to see how they do it.*

Chapter 3

FIND THE DECISION MAKER

Over the years I have learned finding the true decision maker saves you time, money, and a lot of headaches. When I began offering my "Marketing to New Residents" program, I worked hard on targeting local business owners. I started testing my program by targeting auto repair centers. My mailings were directed at the auto repair center owners, because they were the ones opening and reading the mail. I was getting to the decision maker and it was relatively easy to get the owner's name for my *direct mail* pieces.

TOOLBOX TIP

Want to see a sample of a successful prospective script?

Go to www.patpendergast.com, register if you are a first time customer and enter the word "script" in Pendy's Toolbox.

After having somewhat limited success, I decided to expand my program and target dentists. I reasoned dentists have a higher customer lifetime value and very few dentists market their practices correctly. I put together four *direct mail* pieces personalized to the dentist. Two of these *direct mail* pieces were an invitation-sized card with an outer envelope and a compelling offer inside. The other two were postcards with money back guarantees and compelling offers. As I am a big fan of testing, I made sure to send to different mailing lists and split my test between the east and west coast. They ALL bombed! I didn't receive one call or get one hit on my website. Ouch!!

At my business owner's mastermind meetings I got a lot of feedback on the design and message of the mailers. All was good feedback, but I still was not getting response to my mailings. A great suggestion made to me was to interview a dentist to find out how they think. I had been throwing this idea around for a while so this suggestion finally motivated me to move forward. I tried to get a meeting with my dentist, but he backed out as I think he thought I was going to sell him something. I should have presented it as an interview, which I believe he would have then accepted. I tried a different approach and took a dentist friend of mine out to lunch. He owns two practices, so I knew he would offer me invaluable advice. What a gold mine this meeting was! I should have met with him right away. He told me most dentists don't open their own mail. The office manager screens it. If you can convince the office manager, you have your foot in the door. His suggestion was to bribe the office manager with a $5.00 gift card to Starbucks. The token gift makes them feel guilty if they don't take your call. I was on my way to getting my foot in the door. Now I simply had to target my message to appease the office manager, so I could get the message to the dentist.

With the approval from my dentist friend, I tested the Starbucks idea on his office manager. She was given a heads-up I was going to send her something, but wasn't informed as to what I was sending. I sent her a personalized card from my Send-Out Cards account with the outside of the envelope having her name and title of office manager on it. Inside was a $5.00 gift card from Starbucks. I followed up a couple of days after she received the card. She shared her thoughts with me. She felt the card was too plain. If she hadn't known the card was coming from me, she would have thrown it away without opening it. She said the card needed to say gift card enclosed in big letters on an angle in color. She also felt there was too much information on the inside of the card.

Incorporating the office manager's ideas, I made some changes on the outside of the envelope. Keep in mind however; Send-Out Cards has standardized the outside of their envelopes, so it is very difficult to modify it. So, what I did was address the card to "Gift Card Enclosed for: First name of the office manager." I tested again with 10 cards of this design. I called all of the office managers to whom I mailed. I found the cards were still not getting to the correct person, nor were they getting opened. My hands were tied. I couldn't make any modifications to the envelope to make it stand out more.

At my next business owner's mastermind meeting I explained the difficulty I was having. Kevin Kowalke, the facilitator, said I should send a box of brownies. Hard to miss a box of brownies right?! Send-Out Cards has a gift program with gourmet brownies and cookies you can send. So with some help from my marketing savvy friend James Schaefer, I completely re-wrote the card going along with the brownies. I sent my first box of brownies the same day James gave me his suggestions (fast implementation on a small test market). After a month of mailing brownies to dental office business managers, I have deemed it a success. I am able to get the attention of the office manager and they take my calls.

🔥 HOT TIP

Want to find great Lumpy Mail ideas?

Visit 3DMailResults.com to see the latest products my friend Travis Lee has.

When I call the decision maker, I ask if I can show him/her how to bring in more patients. 90% of the time I get a yes, which triggers the sending of a big yellow envelope containing samples of the marketing invitation and a zip code request form. The big yellow envelope stands out in the mail pile, so when I call the office manager back and ask if he/she received the "Big Yellow Envelope" he/she knows exactly what I'm talking about. This gives me leverage to further discuss the program and get the dental business on board.

The final piece of the puzzle is still eluding me. How do I get to the actual dentist and get their final approval? My tactic has been to entice the office manager and get him/her convinced this is the program for their office. It is difficult however to utilize the office manager as a salesperson in front of the dentist. The closing of the process is out of my hands and has caused a number of road blocks to pop up in my way.

My business owner's mastermind group discussed sending a small plastic trash can with a handwritten (not really, but it looks like it is) letter inside. The letter opens by telling the dentist I've done him/her the favor of throwing this letter in the trash, so he/she might as well read it. The letter goes on to tell the dentist a story about success and asks why he/she hasn't signed up for the program. Continuing to test, I also have a second letter using zip code counts and actual numbers showing patient revenue and potential sales volume. I will test the story approach and the number approach to see which works best.

Sales and marketing is one big test, constantly evolving. I share my dentist example as of way of showing you I never consider myself finished in any of my sales and marketing programs. In order to be successful I have to be fluid and flexible. It is my intention to show you the importance of testing and measuring, as well as figuring out who the true decision maker is within your prospective client office or group.

Mailing Lists

The success of your *direct mail* campaign will hinge on the accuracy of the mail list targeting the proper demographic. The most overlooked list, which is actually quite important, is your current client list. Are you sending something to your clients in the mail at least once a month? These people have already purchased from you and are ready to do business with you again. It is important for you to stay in touch with them on a regular basis. You cannot use a shotgun approach, hitting or missing sporadically with your customers. Consistency keeps you top of mind and maintains customer loyalty. Tell your customers what is new or going on in your business. Share how these things will benefit them. You'll find the response rate will be the highest with this group if you remain consistent.

HOT TIP

I have found that infoUSA.com has really good mailing lists.

Real World Experience

Mark Berman and Son, of Mequon, WI, is an independent clothier catering to high-end clients. They are great at sending *direct mail* to current clients and at getting fantastic results with this consistent contact.

Here are some examples of the types of mailings they do:

- Mail out a postcards with holiday hours during the Christmas season.

- A postcard announcement they will be closed on a Friday to reprice all clothing.

- A postcard announcement of a name brand sale. This is an important one. Berman will get reimbursed from the manufacturer for co-op advertising. This is a great way to lower your cost of your *direct mail* program as some companies will rebate the cost of the whole program. Make sure to investigate this little gold nugget.

- A postcard announcement of a women's only event. Berman will target a mailing to the female-only part of the list. Berman has the list in excel and can sort the list based on men, women or all.

- A postcard announcement of a "silly sale". Any other excuse to announce a sale has been very effective for them.

On average, they will have a mailing every month going to current and past customers. Since this type of advertising is so successful, they do not use any other type of advertising.

⚙️🔧 TOOLBOX TIP

Want to see a sample of a postcard?
Go to www.patpendergast.com, register if you are a first time customer and enter the word "berman" in Pendy's Toolbox.

Understanding your customer

It is very important for you to know who your customer is. The correct demographic will help you establish your targets. The more information you have, the better the list you can purchase, and the higher the success rate of your mailing. If I am selling diapers, I don't want to have a list of 50 plus year-old males. I want to target 20 – 35 year old females. The more information you have about your customers, the more accurate the list will be at targeting a qualified prospect. Doing your work ahead of time will increase your bottom line.

SUMMARY

- *Make sure you know who the decision-maker is.*

- *Test, test, test brings you closer to success!*

- *Interview a decision-maker to find out how they think.*

- *Make the gatekeeper happy and remember you.*

- *Know the demographics of your prospect to create an effective mailing list.*

- *Postcards to existing and past customers is a gold mine.*

- *Do you really know who your customer or prospect is?*

Chapter 4
NEWSLETTERS

One of the best ways to stay in front of your customers is with a monthly newsletter. Your newsletter can be very specific to your industry, tailored for your customers with product reviews, or a newsletter talking all about you. My personal favorite and the one I believe is most effective is the latter—a newsletter about you. When you talk about yourself, people will gain an emotional attachment to you and your story. Talking about yourself is very personable and allows you to be vulnerable. When you show your personal side to your customers or prospects, you become more human and, thus; more easily interconnected. Sharing your life in your newsletter forms a special bond with customers--a bond which simply can't be purchased. Be careful, however; don't go overboard bragging or showing off your new vacation home or boat. Customers don't want to see your new toys bought with the profits from their purchases. Talk about more everyday things such as your latest camping trip. Discuss how you had to put your camping food up in a tree to keep it away from bears. Share humorously painful stories such as how Thanksgiving dinner went with the in-laws. Everyone likes a good laugh and can relate to a good story about your father-in-law chasing the dog after it snatched the turkey from the dining room table. Tell funny stories involving you. Heck, if you don't have any, make one up. You're the author and who has to know.

Here are some more ideas regarding stories about you:

Sports	Hobbies	If your dog could talk
Pets	Goals	A Failure you experienced
College	Your Faith	The latest hot topic in the community
Lifestyle	Exercise	What was a life changing event for you
Your Opinion	Heroes	Talk about your Mom and Dad
Favorite gift	A hard lesson	A surprising turn of events
One thing you'd change		Your proudest moment
Family , Kids, Grandkids		A teacher that impacted your life
An awkward social moment		The hardest news you've had to deliver

A book you are reading or a book that changed your life

Your biggest loss (people love to read about someone else experiencing a loss versus bragging about a success, this puts them in your shoes)

No matter how boring you may think your life may be, there is always a story to tell.

Guest Articles

Consider a section of your newsletter reserved for a guest writer. Look around you. There are many people within your circle who are experts in something. There are tons of people wanting to spread a message and are looking for a platform. Keep your eyes open. Once you see an article you like and would enjoy having it in your newsletter, contact the author. It shouldn't cost you anything more than a plug for them and their website. My newsletter has two guest writers. One is a medical doctor specializing in life changing practices for a happier life. The other is a business entrepreneur giving advice on marketing, customer growth, and retention. I am a big fan of self-improvement and motivational writings. Both of these gentlemen bring it. Here are their websites to contact them directly to add to your newsletter:

TheKowalkeGroup.com and *RickSchaeferMD.com*

People writing a blog or a monthly article will love to have their article in your newsletter. It gives them a larger audience to talk to about their passions. Offer to promote their website and contact information in their article. This should be enough payment for them.

Another neat idea is including a recipe from a famous person or celebrity. I feature a recipe each month on the back panel of my newsletter. I have found this recipe cut out and hanging in client's offices. Another idea is to use a customer's or employee's recipe. This gives your newsletter a personal touch.

Email me at pat@welcomecardusa.com to be put on my mailing list and receive my monthly newsletter. You can then swipe and deploy the ideas I am using.

Touchy Subjects

You know what they say about talking politics and religion at a party. Don't do it! Well the same rule holds true for writing in your newsletter. Stay away from subjects alienating you from your audience (your customers). I market to everyone. I stay away from current events possibly causing a customer to disagree with me or worst case, not buy from me. The reason for a newsletter is to promote your business and have your customers get to know you. If you have a very strong opinion about a subject, think about blogging it on a website not in your newsletter. Your newsletter is meant to encourage customers and clients to buy from you. If you make a stand on a subject, half your audience may disagree with you. You want your recipients to like you and buy from you. The last thing you want is for your customer to be on the defensive over a subject having nothing to do with your product. I recently sent out an email blast to my customer base. It was about taxes and contained a quote from Jim Rohn. If you're unfamiliar, Jim Rohn's life is a riches to rags to riches story. Rohn was a millionaire by age 31 in the late 50's. In 1960, Rohn was VP of a company called Nutri-Bio. Nutri-Bio went out of business in early 1960 taking Rohn's net worth from 2.3 million to almost zero. A friend of Rohn's hired him to host recruiting and training meetings all across the country, paying him $250,000 up front. Ultimately

Rohn presented seminars, worldwide, for more than 40 years. Jim Rohn mentored the likes of Tony Robbins, Mark Victor Hansen and Jack Canfield to name a few. His teachings are rooted in faith and the goodness in all people. If you help enough people become successful, you will follow.

🔥 HOT TIP

For great motivation and sales info, go to JimRohn.com. Be sure to sign up for his free email newsletter.

Getting It Done

Newsletters consume lots of time. Just getting an article every month from someone can be very difficult and time consuming. It has been my experience getting a short article done monthly is easier. I write the rough draft and my wife edits it for content and grammar, which is very helpful for me. Here is a tip: find a company in your industry producing newsletters. Find a company willing to give you a template of the artwork so you can make your own changes. This allows you to personalize the newsletter and stay away from a stock look. This will help you get the newsletter done each month as it's easier for you to only have to write a small article to complete the newsletter and get it out the door. If you feel you can produce your own newsletter, great. Just keep in mind to allot time each month to get it completed. My newsletter is "canned," which means it comes to me ready to print. All I have to do is put in my masthead and date. Over the years, I have customized my newsletter with guest articles and my own personal stories. Readership and comments have gone up considerably since I have made it more personal.

Format for Newsletters

Your budget is going to dictate the type of newsletter you will have. Expect this to be your first big roadblock. You may spend days or weeks thinking of a great layout with color and pictures, etc.... Stop. The key in the beginning is simply to get something in the mail and improve on it each month. I have seen customers try time and time again to come up with the perfect newsletter the first time. Don't waste the time and energy perfecting your newsletter. Start with a simple first issue and improve on it each time thereafter. Improving a newsletter is fun and you will look forward to the challenge each month. Your first one can be 8.5 x 11, black and white on two sides, folded to letter size, taped shut and mailed with a stamp. Hooray! You've published your first newsletter and gotten in front of your customer, helping you to gain the top of mind position for when your customer decides to buy your product. If you're Microsoft savvy, you can consider improving your newsletter using the program called Microsoft Publisher. Honestly, I am a big advocate of purchasing a "canned" newsletter service over spending the time creating your own. Here are my reasons:

1. Time. Your time is better spent on your business than spending hours writing and creating your newsletter.

2. Quality. A newsletter service will produce a better product than you can--unless of course you are a graphic artist who majored in English.

3. Get it done. By subscribing to a newsletter service, you put the monthly pressure on them to write the newsletter, put it together, create the art, and package it up for delivery to their customers. This will also help you avoid missing a month or two.

4. Consistency is key. No hit or miss. People will start to expect your newsletter and will look forward to reading it.

Picture with your Dog

We are all acquainted with a pet lover. Whether a cat, horse, lizard, rat or dog, pet lovers can be totally obsessed with their animals. Some value a pet more than a child. Put your pet's picture in the newsletter and tell the readers a little about it. In fact, if you are a dog owner, I encourage you to have a picture of you with your dog included in your newsletter. You may even want to have it in all your marketing materials. The public relates to a dog owner very strongly. Reader response rates increase when a person is pictured with his/her dog. Readers connect with the person and trust him/her more quickly. What an easy way to gain the trust of your customers! Here is an idea, if you don't have a dog, borrow one. Who has to know it's not yours. Just be ready for some detailed questions. Use your neighbor's dog and name him the company mascot. Have some fun. You may be surprised at the response.

Swipe and Deploy

Are there any original marketing ideas left in this world? Many of the *direct mail* pieces you see are old ideas repackaged into today's colors and lingo. If you go back 30 or more years and look at the ads in newspapers or magazines, you'll see familiar content. The only things changed are price, color, and an increase in consumer goods for sale. You should be scanning your mail every day to see what is being done by other industries and by your competitors. Does their marketing message get your attention? Do they have a compelling offer? Is there a deadline? Does a particular marketing piece catch your eye because of its shape or color? If you like it, why not use it?

I have been taking other people's ideas and incorporating them into my *direct mail* campaigns for years. We call this the swipe and deploy technique. Take someone else's idea and improve on it. Just be careful you don't use copy written material and always get permission from the author before using the material.

The previous example of sending Starbucks cards to dental office managers as a ploy of instilling guilt for unanswered phone calls is an example of using the swipe and deploy method. I took this idea to the next level and sent a small box of brownies. It got the attention of the office managers, and they remembered me when I called. This is a great example of swipe and deploy and improving on an idea.

Here is a newsletter example of swipe and deploy. Instead of using just a normal type font, why not use your own handwriting? I had my handwriting turned into a font, so I can convert any article I write into my personal script. This is another way of endearing your customer to you with a personal touch. I typically only use my handwriting font on the front page article of my newsletter. I find this simple touch acts as an ideal opener to the rest of my publication. Adding variety will get a better response rate.

🔥 HOT TIP

Go to SendOutCards.com

This company has a method of staying in touch with customers and friends. It is automated and allows you to send gifts as well.

SUMMARY

- *Newsletters get you in front of your customer on a regular basis.*

- *Make your newsletter personal, show them your vulnerability.*

- *Tap your business friends for articles.*

- *Stay away from religion and politics.*

- *Purchase a newsletter template.*

- *People love dogs.*

- *Repackage old ideas.*

- *Add variety.*

Chapter 5
TESTING

It would be fantastic if everytime we came up with a new marketing idea it worked. Unfortunately, in the real world this isn't the case. In the real world, your best chance at success is through measuring your results for accurate information. You can't simply trust your gut instinct. You have to measure your results. If your results aren't on paper showing how many people responded to your offer, it simply doesn't count as valid measurement.

A great example of needing measurement is yellow page ads. Two easy methods to track the effectiveness of your yellow page ad are:

1. Have a special phone number listed and keep track of calls to that number

2. Have all your staff ask the caller how they found you.

Test these methods to give yourself the type of information you need to make a yellow page ad decision.

Let's be honest, can you give me concrete numbers as to how many people are calling from your yellow page ad? I didn't think so. If you really want to be in the yellow pages, just put in a line listing with your phone number and address and be done with it. Most of the time, those are discount shoppers looking for the cheapest price and not the quality customer you want.

5 Ways to get a Response

1. Direct Mail Testing

Direct mail is one of the easiest methods with which to do testing. For easy comparisons, let's take a mailing list of 1000 and split it in half. You want to see the response you get for a 15% discount on a service worth $500.00 to 500 recipients. Mail the other 500 a 25% discount on a service worth $500.00. You may think you will get a better response on the 25% discount, but will you? I'm not looking for gut feelings here. Gut feelings don't put money in your bank account. Prove it. Measure the results. You may be surprised to get the same response rate at 15% as the 25% discount. Your results will determine what works best for you. Get rid of the guessing and get proven results. Then you can make a decision on how to spend your marketing dollars most effectively.

2. Lumpy Mail (Dimensional Mail)

Lumpy mail is just that—lumpy. You can physically feel it. You have something lumpy in an envelope causing curiosity so it gets opened. Lumpy mail can help you stand out from the crowd and get your foot in the door. If you have received a pen in the mail from one of those pen companies, then you know what lumpy mail looks and feels like. This has worked for the pen companies for years and tells you it will work for you too. Lumpy mail is a bit more expensive and I suggest you really nail down your demographics and get your mailing list as targeted as possible before embarking on a lumpy mail campaign. To find all the lumpy mail ideas and products you will need, go to 3dmailresults.com. Travis Lee has been doing this for years and is an industry expert.

⚙ TOOLBOX TIP

Want to see a sample of a successful "Lumpy Mail" campaign?

Go to www.patpendergast.com, register if you are a first time customer and enter the word "lumpy" in Pendy's Toolbox.

3. Brownie Experiment

In my Welcome Card USA business, we try to get to the decision maker in a dental office so they will take our call. The decision maker happens to be the office manager, and I was testing a rather large lumpy mail program. This is where Send-Out Cards is convenient. They offer the ability to send delicious Gourmet Foods. I designed a card to go on top of a box of 4 brownies mailed to the office manager. I've been told by dental office managers most mail gets thrown out if it looks remotely similar to junk mail. So how can they not open a box coming to them via the United States Post Office? After they receive this in the mail, I call and ask to speak to the office manager and ask them if they liked the brownies? After taking my call and a little chit chat, I get into my pitch, which is what will ultimately make me the profit. Lumpy mail is a more expensive method, but will get you through to the hard to reach prospects. Your return on investment will show you in the long run lumpy mail isn't such an expensive program.

⚙ TOOLBOX TIP

Want to see a sample of what the brownie box looks like?

Go to www.patpendergast.com, register if you are a first time customer and enter the word "brownie" in Pendy's Toolbox.

4. Handwritten Notes

What is amazing to me is some of the "Old School" methods of communication are still as effective, if not more, in these days of electronic communication. One of the most overlooked techniques of effective communication is the old-fashioned handwritten note. When was the last time you received a handwritten note in the mail? If and when you did, did it get your attention? I'm sure it did. I'm sure you also recognize when a birthday card arrives in your mailbox with simply a happy birthday and a signature. It's not nearly as powerful or personal as an actual handwritten message inside the card. If you want to be remembered by your customer, go the extra mile. You'll find your customer going out of his or her way to thank you and possibly even proudly display your card on his/ her desk or refrigerator. How's that for staying "top of mind" with a customer?

Here is a real world example of the power of a handwritten note. Our local girl's high school coach was the television commentator for the girl's state basketball final. My wife and I watched the game and commented afterward about how good a job the coach had done. I decided to write a note to her and congratulate her on her successful commentating. A couple of months later I saw her in the store and the first thing she said to me was how wonderful it was to get my note in the mail. She shared how she kept the note. I'm sure not many people sent her a handwritten note. She will remember what I did for a long time.

Here is my secret method of sending out at least 10 cards a day. I use Send-Out Cards. This company has a staple of stock cards from which you can choose. You can then personalize each card. I went a little further and had my handwriting made into a font along with having my signature scanned so I can "sign" each card with my name. When people receive a card from me, they think I actually wrote it out by hand. What is great about this program is it can be used as a customer database to keep track of information about your customers. I can enter the name of the customer, company, all phone numbers, email address, important dates to remember (i.e. birthday, anniversary, purchase date of product), spouse, children, action log (gives me a history of when and what I wrote), and a note section to add extra things to remember. As I have a hard time remembering what I had for lunch yesterday, this keeps me very organized and allows me to send many notes to the same person without repeating my message. Send-out cards offers much more, but these are the features I find very effective.

TOOLBOX TIP

Want to see a sample of a card with my handwriting font?

Go to www.patpendergast.com, register if you are a first time customer and enter the phrase "pat invite" in Pendy's Toolbox.

5. Trash Can Mailer

My good friend Bill Driscol from DeTech turned me onto this *direct mail* eye-catcher. I purchased 20 small plastic trash cans from Bill standing no taller than 4" tall. In fact, Bill mailed me one as an example to show me how they come through. Inside the one Bill mailed me was a letter crumpled up on yellow paper. It was handwritten and it started with, "Dear Pat, Since you have already thrown my 3 previously sent reports into the trash, I decided to send you this note sealed in a trash can. Wait! Before you actually throw this one away PLEASE give me one more chance to explain." The letter goes on to say he is at his son's baseball scrimmage and had some free time to think.

I really like this idea as I want to be able to get the attention of the dentists to whom I am targeting with my mailings. I have another method/letter shared with me from the Owner of Zap Innovations. In it was a cover letter with a very similar message. "I decided to throw this letter out since you have not returned my phone calls or responded to my mailings…." One difference with the Zap Innovations approach was the trash can included another letter explaining the actual profits achievable using the *direct mail*. The additional letter is a real attention-grabber as the numbers can be quite large. Here is an example I used in one of my dentist trash can mailers.

- 535 new residents move into your 6 zip codes each month

- Using the projection of 1.5 – 6 new clients per month of 1000 invitations mailed

- Total lifetime Value Revenue projection = $33,705 to $134,820

- Total Cost of Welcome Card USA mailing = $12,904

These are very powerful numbers and can move a client who is on the fence regarding *direct mail*.

🔥 HOT TIP

If your ROI is large enough, try having a real garbage can delivered to the prospect!
That will get their attention.

Things Not Working - Testing

One of the things I have learned in my business owner's mastermind group and with working the Dan Kennedy systems is the need for testing. One of my strengths is my tenacity to not give up. I have been dealt many set-backs in my life, but the one constant is my ability to not give up. My Welcome Card business is my testament to this. I have been working on this business model since 2005. It can be said I haven't given the time it takes to make this a million dollar business. They say you need at least 10,000 hours to become a success. This equates to 8 hours a day for 3 and a half years of non-stop practice or testing. No breaks! I don't think I have put in the time yet. In fact, I know I haven't tested enough.

Here are some pitfalls I've had in regards to my testing. I share them with you as an example of what not to do. Please learn from my mistakes so you can grow your business more quickly.

🔥 HOT TIP

**Don't forget to include your
current customers in your mailing.**

You will be rewarding them with your offer as a "Thank You".

When I first started my business I sent large packets of information to auto repair shops. I sent thousands at a time. I thought I was following Jim Stratton's (sold me his *direct mail* to dentists program) system. I didn't even keep track of the costs involved in doing this. The postage alone cost me thousands of dollars. When I was able to talk to Jim about what I was doing, he had me stop and send postcards instead. The packets I sent out were supposed to go to prospects who contacted me after mailing them a postcard.

Learn from mistakes and seek advice!

The next method I tried was to send small black and white postcards with a passcode to auto repair shops. The idea was the recipient would go to a website and enter a passcode to watch a video. The reason for the passcode was it would identify who was watching the video. If they watched the video and didn't fill out the information form, I wouldn't know who logged into the website. I would then send them a packet of information with a follow-up call. I got a few hits on the website, but not enough to say the system worked for this type of product.

A floor-covering client of mine wanted to mail a postcard to the households in his general selling area with incomes of $40,000 or more. He designed the postcard, had me supply the mailing list, and finished the mailing. After receiving the finished cards, I noticed some details were missing and would not help his ROI. He didn't have a phone number to call, number to fax to, or a website to visit. These are the minimum needed on a postcard. Heck, if all you did was mail a postcard with these three things on it, you would get someone to respond if only just to ask what was supposed to be on the card! There were a few other helpful items, but it was too late for changes. Needless to say, the card had a very small response rate. This is how *direct mail* gets a bad rap. A company will do a one-time mailing and just throw an offer out there to see what happens. When nothing happens, they are the first to say *direct mail* doesn't work, but they are also the ones having a large ad in the yellow pages and cannot tell you how many calls or sales they get.

A few suggestions for improvement would be to include these methods to contact the company: phone, fax, website, email. You want it to be very easy to reach out for questions. I would also suggest breaking the mailing into 1000 piece increments and having different offers on each. A simple split between a percentage discount, dollar discount, and a one-day-only special would give you a chance to see if one method gets a better response than another. Keep the graphic clutter on the card to a minimum. Keep it easy to read. Finally, I recommend mailing to your past clients. You never know when they will want your product again. It also gives them a chance to tell their friends and family. These few changes will help your *direct mail* piece have a better success rate.

SUMMARY

- *Are you measuring your yellow page ad response rate?*

- *Prove your gut feel with split testing.*

- *Lumpy mail gets opened.*

- *Handwritten notes will set you apart from everyone else.*

- *Mail a trashcan?*

- *Do you know the lifetime value of your customer?*

- *Learn fast from failed tests.*

Chapter 6
TRACKING YOUR RESULTS

It is very important to track the results of your *direct mail* campaign. You should test and retest to determine what works the best for your business. Anything you do for marketing should be tracked whether it's a postcard, invitation or newspaper ad. It's impossible to determine if a marketing piece is valuable if you don't track and measure the results.

In my Welcome Card *direct mail* program, my clients are given a tracking report of names and addresses for each mailing so they can track results. Tracking is also the best way to see which offer or type of piece gets different results. You may think your 25% discount off a purchase may be giving you great results. But you should test to see if a 20% or 15% discount gives you the same result, thus; costing you less and making you more profitable. Without measuring results, it is impossible to tell which offer is working.

The following is a sample tracking report given to my *direct mail* clients. It is an easy way for them to track their response rate to the monthly mailing. This is easily cross-referenced in their accounting system.

Sample Tracking Report

Welcome Card USA®

New Customer Acquisition
Invitation Tracking Report
August 2013
Custom Compiled for: Precision Automotive Services

	LAST NAME	FIRST NAME	STREET ADDRESS	CITY	ST	ZIP	RESPONSE DATE
1	ACHTERHOF	VIRGINIA	17007 FENNY BRIDGE LN	SPRING	TX	77379	
2	ADAMS	GWENDOLYN	2731 HONEYSUCKLE WALK	SPRING	TX	77388	
3	ADAMS	SANDRA	20211 POST OAK HILL DR	SPRING	TX	77388	
4	AKIRI	JULIE	3902 SUNSTONE DR	HOUSTON	TX	77068	
5	ALCOCER	BONIA	3603 CHARWOOD CT	HOUSTON	TX	77068	
6	ALTUNIAN	RUBEN	9542 ENSTONE CIR	SPRING	TX	77379	
7	AMMONS	JESSE	16911 MARKRIDGE DR	SPRING	TX	77379	
8	AMOS	CHARLES	5514 COBBLE LN	SPRING	TX	77379	
9	AMRANI	ROI	122 W NORTH HILL DR	SPRING	TX	77388	

Keeping track of your response rate is extremely important for a couple of reasons.

1. It gives you your ROI (return on investment discussed in later chapter) numbers.

2. It tells you how many people are responding to your mailing.

3. It can tell you the demographic of your mailing, thus; letting you concentrate on your target audience.

4. It can tell you if you are pricing incorrectly or selling the wrong item.

5. Allows you to follow up with a more direct and personalized mailing to the prospect.

How to Track Response Rate

This is the hard part. Getting your staff to ask the person on the phone or at the front counter how or why they have contacted your business. It is a simple question and worth its weight in gold. Unfortunately, I have seen this simple question bypassed way too many times. The person answering the phone is not trained to ask this important question, or is embarrassed to ask. I can't stress this enough. Make sure you and your staff make it a habit to ask how the customer found you.

Recently, I was in a client's office when they took a phone call. After they hung up, I asked how the caller found you? Oops, they forgot to ask even with me standing directly in front of them. It starts from the top and has to be enforced. I have an appliance repair dealer whose staff is very good at asking how the caller found them. Since they also are on the radio and TV, it is important for them to find out what method of advertising is working, and this information gives them hard facts on results.

TOOLBOX TIP

Want to see a sample of a tracking method?

Go to www.patpendergast.com, register if you are a first time customer and enter the phrase "track it" in Pendy's Toolbox.

I have used another method of tracking results by incorporating the internet. On one of my *direct mail* postcards I directed the recipient to a website. In order to enter the site the recipient had to enter a passcode from the postcard. The magic of this method was the passcode was matched up to specific mailing lists and customer ID. I knew instantly who the visitor was. I was able to call and follow-up with multiple mailings to this prospect.

A feature many software programs use is the ability to track customers in a sortable database. Please check with your software supplier to see what is available and how to use it. This is often one of the most underutilized part of a software program and can be a powerful marketing tool.

Come up with your own script sheet for placement by each phone.

The script doesn't have to be complicated, but will assist your employees. Keep a tally sheet by each phone as well. It can be very simple and easy to use. The crucial pieces needed for tracking purposes are:

- Date

- Phone, in-person or online customer

- How did customer hear about your business

- Product purchased

This simple information gives you a way to track how many people responded to a mailing from the date of the response. You also have what was purchased, giving you the sales amount. This is all part of your ROI equation.

ROI (Return on Investment)

Many of us thought justifying the results of our *direct mail* campaign meant having a 2% response rate. Not sure who determined this figure, but I think it is the wrong way to measure the results of your campaign.

The best way to measure the effectiveness or success of your *direct mail* campaign is to use return on investment (ROI). ROI will give you the numbers needed to determine how much a customer is worth (profit) and how much you can invest (spend) in converting a prospect into a customer.

The numbers in the graph to follow show the potential profit for every dollar invested. I use this flyer when I speak with dentists. It's is a great way to visualize the impact of response rates to results.

Test different offers to measure response rates. You may get a great response rate on one of your offers, but the offer may have a low margin rate. You may be more successful with an offer getting a lower response rate, but has a higher profit margin. Sometimes fewer people through the door with a high profit transaction is more successful than many people through the door stressing staff and facilities. Just think what a Groupon offer would do to your business--low profit, high stress, upset employees and unsatisfied customers.

Here is the money making math...

New Resident Marketing Profit Projections

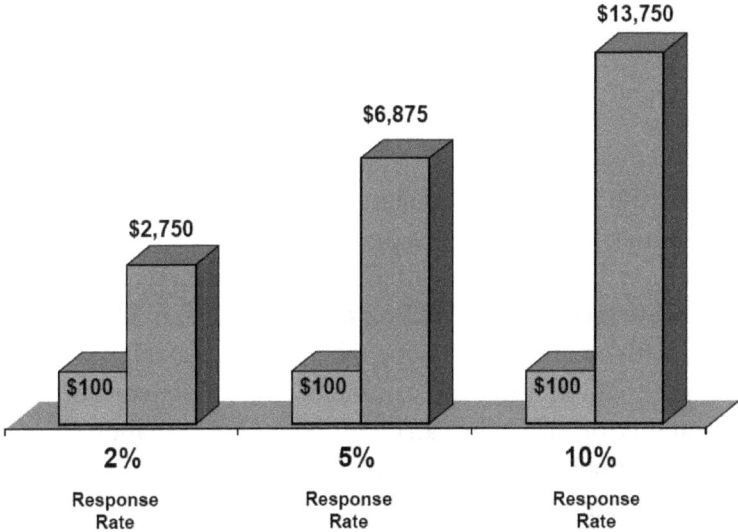

	$13,750
$6,875	
$2,750	
$100	$100	$100
2%	**5%**	**10%**
Response Rate	Response Rate	Response Rate

Return on Investment for every $100 you invest in marketing to New Residents

The profit projections shown above are based on the following industry statistics; The average "customer lifespan" in the automotive service business is 5-7 years during which time a customer will spend between $2100-$3700. The average customer household has 1.8 vehicles.

The New Resident Profit Projections above use an average customer value of $2500 – you can adjust this figure up or done for your shop.

Case Studies

A great example of a business returning to *direct mail* is Cinnabon. Cinnabon's 750 mall stores relied on their location within the mall and their delicious aroma of baking cinnamon buns to drive business in. It was a sufficient strategy until the recession hit. Foot traffic dropped precipitously and the spontaneous purchase of Cinnabons declined. Enter *direct mail*. Cinnabon decided to insert oversized coupon sheets in the Money Mailer's business to business package, sent to small businesses within 2-mile radius of the store location. The result was a 4.6% response and positive ROI.

Val-Pak, Money Mailer and other merge-mail systems offer very low delivery cost and high open rates. More businesses and a greater variety of businesses ought to be using such merge-mail systems.

Don't miss the fact of the non-standard piece mailer itself in this case. A non-standard piece is a postcard larger than letter size, which is 11 ½ " long by 6 1/8" high. In the following case, Money Mailer's CEO credited the "billboard piece" which is a 8" x 12" postcard with coupons for having a higher success rate and positive ROI. If a cinnamon bun shop can make *direct mail* work with its small transaction size, why can't you? Note the Cinnabon shop owner didn't mail to consumers, he mailed B2B, and thus; reached clumps of consumers. He couldn't afford *direct mail* to get Mom in to buy a cinnamon bun, so he rearranged the target.

Make it your goal to get back to precision targeted marketing this year. It may seem more expensive and absent of appropriate strategy. If you know your customer demographic, response rate and ROI, you can create a more expensive mailing with better results. Waiting for folks to come in because the aroma of your bakery is cheaper and is a sheer way to a dying business.

SUMMARY

- *Testing different offers and tracking the results is better than a gut feel.*

- *Tracking results identifies your ROI.*

- *Your staff needs to track calls and visits.*

- *Script incoming calls.*

- *Know your ROI.*

- *Be precise with your direct mail marketing.*

Lets continue the Journey...

If you enjoyed this book and want to continue to learn new ideas and techniques, visit my website at PatPendergast.com. This is the best way for me to stay in touch with you, my clients, prospects, and friends to tell them about new and exciting methods to grow your business. I encourage you to sign up for my monthly newsletter. Besides the vast amount of content it has, it may give you ideas for your newsletter. I encourage you to "swipe and deploy" my ideas!

Email me at Pat@MillPM.com, with the word NEWSLETTER in the subject line, and be sure to include your mailing address. If you are interested in having a motivational quote emailed to you twice a week, email me at Pat@MillPM.com with MOTIVATION in the subject line.

I challenge you to implement one new marketing idea this week. Take one of the ideas that I shared with you in this book and get it in the mail. I want you to be successful with your business, but nothing will happen unless you act today.

Continued Success!

Pat Pendergast

Acknowledgements

for my kids **Christopher**, **Jordy**, & **Bridget**
and my amazing wife, **Cathy**
Who I'm doing it all for with love

for my brother, **Paul**
My source of daily inspiration

for **Kevin Kowalke** & **Tim Schmidt**
My coaches and mentors

for my mother-in-law, **Bobbie**
The first author in our family who inspired me

for my father-in-law, **FT**
*The ultimate sales person who taught me that
sales is the best profession in the world*

for the **"Nite Riders"**
*The morning rides give me the energy
and motivation to do more*

for my **Dad**
*Who instilled in me the hard work ethic
and dependability I have today*

In Loving Memory of my Mom & Aunt Connie

www.ingramcontent.com/pod-product-compliance
Lightning Source LLC
Chambersburg PA
CBHW070357200326
41518CB00012B/2262